'Great poems,' David Whyte has said, 'are not about experience, but are the experience itself, felt in the body.' *Essentials* is a collection of his own best poems, each in their way about capturing the experience itself, whether that is in the daily shifts, the ever-turning seasons or the bigger cycle of gain and grief that are part of our journey through life. Each poem is accompanied by a short context on where and when it was written. Together they form an elegant testament to David Whyte's most closely-held understanding – that human life cannot be apportioned out as one thing or another; rather, it is best seen as a living conversation, a way between and beyond, made beautiful by darkness as well as light, at its essence both deeply solitary and profoundly communal.

This updated edition includes poems from his 2021 collection, *Still Possible*.

ESSENTIALS

ESSENTIALS

POEMS AND
A CONSOLATION

DAVID WHYTE

CANONGATE

First published in Great Britain in 2022
by Canongate Books Ltd, 14 High Street, Edinburgh EH1 1TE

First published in the USA in 2020 by
Many Rivers Press, PO Box 868, Langley, WA 98260

canongate.co.uk

2

British Library Cataloguing-in-Publication Data
A catalogue record for this book is available on
request from the British Library

ISBN 978 1 83885 812 4

Printed and bound by CPI (UK) Ltd, Croydon CR0 4YY

FSC
www.fsc.org

MIX
Paper | Supporting
responsible forestry
FSC® C171272

Nel mezzo del cammin di nostra vita
Mi ritrovai per una selva oscura,
Che la diritta via era smarrita.

In the middle of the road of our life
I awoke in a dark wood,
Where the true way was wholly lost

DANTE ALIGHIERI
The Inferno
Canto 1, line 1
Trans DW

Contents

Introduction

The act of writing anything worthwhile always takes place at that strange and sometimes disturbing cross-roads where aloneness and intimacy meet. The solitariness of the writer, sometimes at a desk, sometimes while writing in a notebook on a skittering knee while travelling, always, if followed rightly, culminates in a radical form of undoing that leads to the distinctions between aloneness and togetherness breaking down altogether. This break of the boundary between what we think is a self and what we think is other than our self is where the rich vein of beauty and insight becomes a reward in and of itself, and where the words suddenly seem to belong to everyone.

It is all the more satisfying a reward then, to see this essential collection of thoughts and writings, written in so many different circumstances, over so many years, both at home and in so many far places, gathered and brought together by one very close and dear intimate, in the form of my wife and partner, Gayle Karen Young Whyte. It is a double pleasure to have the book designed in collaboration by two very good, very close friends: companions in artistry and in the mountains, Edward Wates and John Neilson. I consider it a great measure of any success in life that those so close to me could remain ardent supporters of the essence of my work over so many years: respect and support always being the necessary bedrock of any good marriage or any real friendship.

Speaking of friendship, one of the many ways we have made ourselves lonely without gaining the deeper nourishment and intimacies of true aloneness, is the way we have lost the greater supporting circle of friendship available to us in the created, natural world: to be friends with the sky, the rain, the changing light of a given day and the horizon always leading us beyond the circle we have drawn too readily for ourselves. This book is, in many ways, a celebration of the wider circle of friendship that is our birthright. It is in wishing to deepen and make more intimate, and to live into and up to the consequences of that rich relationship with our world and our astonishing planet, and in posing all the beautiful questions that this world asks of us, that much of this work has been written.

DAVID WHYTE
Langley
August 2019

Start Close In

Start close in,
don't take the second step
or the third,
start with the first
thing
close in,
the step
you don't want to take.

Start with
the ground
you know,
the pale ground
beneath your feet,
your own
way to begin
the conversation.

Start with your own
question,
give up on other
people's questions,
don't let them
smother something
simple.

To hear
another's voice,
follow
your own voice,

wait until
that voice
becomes an
intimate private ear
that can
really listen
to another.

Start right now
take a small step
you can call your own
don't follow
someone else's
heroics, be humble
and focused,
start close in,
don't mistake
that other
for your own.

Start close in,
don't take
the second step
or the third,
start with the first
thing
close in,
the step
you don't want to take.

START CLOSE IN   *This poem was inspired by the first lines of Dante's* Comedia, *written in the midst of the despair of exile from his beloved Florence. It reflects the difficult act we all experience, of trying to make a home in the world again when everything has been taken away; the necessity of stepping bravely again, into what looks now like a dark wood, when the outer world as we know it has disappeared, when the world has to be met and in some ways made again from no outer ground but from the very center of our being. The temptation is to take the second or third step, not the first, to ignore the invitation into the center of our own body, into our grief, to attempt to finesse the grief and the absolutely necessary understanding at the core of the pattern, to forgo the radical and almost miraculous simplification into which we are being invited. Start close in.*

The Journey

Above the mountains
    the geese turn into
      the light again

painting their
    black silhouettes
      on an open sky.

Sometimes everything
    has to be
      inscribed across
        the heavens

so you can find
    the one line
      already written
        inside you.

Sometimes it takes
    a great sky
      to find that

first, bright
    and indescribable
      wedge of freedom
        in your own heart.

Sometimes with
    the bones of the black
        sticks left when the fire
            has gone out

someone has written
    something new
        in the ashes of your life.

You are not leaving.
    Even as the light fades quickly now,
        you are arriving.

THE JOURNEY *There is every reason to despair due to all the present events that seem out of our control, but there is every reason to hope that with attention and discipline, we can bring ourselves and our societies, through a kind of necessary seasonal disappearance, back into the realm of choice.*

Firstly, the easy part: despair. The world at present seems to be a mirror to many of our worst qualities. We could not have our individual fears and prejudices, our wish to feel superior to others, and our deep desire not to be touched by the heartbreak and vulnerabilities that accompany every life, more finely drawn and better represented in the outer world than are presented to us now, by the iconic and often ugly political figures, encouraging the worst in their fellows that dominate our screens and our times.

Life is fierce and difficult. There is no life we can live without being subject to grief, loss and heartbreak. Half of every conversation is mediated through disappearance. Thus, there is every reason to want to retreat from life, to carry torches that illuminate only our own view, to make enemies of life and of others, to hate what we cannot understand and to keep the world and the people who inhabit it at a distance through prejudicial naming; but therefore, it also follows, that our ability to do the opposite, to meet the other in the world on their own terms, without diminishing them, is one of the necessary signatures of human courage; and one we are being asked to write, above all our flaws and difficulties, across the heavens of this, our present time. The essence in other words of The Journey.

Sweet Darkness

When your eyes are tired,
the world is tired also.

When your vision has gone,
no part of the world can find you.

Time to go into the dark
where the night has eyes
to recognize its own.

There you can be sure
you are not beyond love.

The dark will be your home
tonight.

The night will give you a horizon
further than you can see.

You must learn one thing.
The world was made to be free in.

Give up all the other worlds
except the one to which you belong.

Sometimes it takes darkness and the sweet
confinement of your aloneness
to learn

anything or anyone
that does not bring you alive

is too small for you.

SWEET DARKNESS *This poem was written out of that very physical and almost breathless giving away most human beings feel when they must let go of what seems most precious to them, not knowing how or when it will return, in what form or in what voice - that taking away of the light, walking through divorce or separation, through bereavement or through simply not recognizing the person looking back at us in the mirror. 'Sweet Darkness' was written in a kind of defiant praise of this difficult time of not knowing, a letter of invitation to embrace the beauty of the night and of the foundational human experience of not being able to see, as actually another horizon, and perhaps the only horizon out of which a truly new revelation can emerge. The last line cuts both ways, of course: we ourselves have often helped to make everything and everyone around us far too small, by our lack of faith in the midst of a necessary not knowing, by all the ways we are not holding the conversation.*

Sometimes

Sometimes
if you move carefully
through the forest,

breathing
like the ones
in the old stories,

who could cross
a shimmering bed of leaves
without a sound,

you come
to a place
whose only task

is to trouble you
with tiny
but frightening requests,

conceived out of nowhere
but in this place
beginning to lead everywhere.

Requests to stop what
you are doing right now,
and

to stop what you
are becoming
while you do it,

questions
that can make
or unmake
a life,

questions
that have patiently
waited for you,

questions
that have no right
to go away.

SOMETIMES *Almost all individual and communal transformations take place, especially at the beginning, almost silently, without announcement or declaration that the season and the way forward have changed irrevocably. Like the first falling leaf at the end of summer that goes unnoticed. 'Sometimes' looks at this constant dynamic of entrance through trepidation, anticipation and slowly growing understanding of the new. As a child I was given a lavishly illustrated book of Native American myths and stories, a book I returned to again and again for years, wearing away the edges of the pages as I did, but out of all the haunting stories and intriguing pictures, one stood out for me, the image of a young boy in a primeval forest being taught by an elder how to cross a piece of broken ground, without making a single sound. I returned to this story repeatedly, I know now out of the child's intuition that we are all moving silently and unannounced, all transiting and maturing into new territories and new dispensations without the essentials of those transitions ever having been explained or spoken; the last line in many respects is the essence of the poet's work, to work with the questions 'that have no right to go away' in the life of an individual, in the life of a relationship or marriage, and in our collective conversations in an increasingly fraught, worldwide society.*

The Winter of Listening

No one but me by the fire,
my hands burning
red in the palms while
the night wind carries
everything away outside.

All this petty worry
while the great cloak
of the sky grows dark
and intense
round every living thing.

What is precious
inside us does not
care to be known
by the mind
in ways that diminish
its presence.

What we strive for
in perfection
is not what turns us
into the lit angel
we desire,

what disturbs
and then nourishes
has everything
we need.

What we hate
in ourselves
is what we cannot know
in ourselves but
what is true to the pattern
does not need
to be explained.

Inside everyone
is a great shout of joy
waiting to be born.

Even with summer
so far off
I feel it grown in me
now and ready
to arrive in the world.

All those years
listening to those
who had
nothing to say.

All those years
forgetting
how everything
has its own voice
to make
itself heard.

All those years
forgetting
how easily
you can belong
to everything
simply by listening.

And the slow
difficulty
of remembering
how everything
is born from
an opposite
and miraculous
otherness.

Silence and winter
have led me to that
otherness.

So let this winter
of listening
be enough
for the new life
I must call my own.

We speak
only with the voices of those
we can hear ourselves

and only for that portion
of the body of the world
it has learned to perceive.

And
here
in the tumult
of the night
I hear the walnut
above the child's swing
swaying its dark limbs
in the wind
and the rain now
come to beat
against my window
and somewhere
in this cold night
of wind and stars
the first whispered
opening of
those hidden
and invisible springs
that uncoil
in the summer air
each yet
to be imagined rose.

THE WINTER OF LISTENING *Within this poem is an ancient intuitive understanding of winter as a time to leave things alone, to let things remain hidden, even to themselves. A time when to name anything would be to give it the wrong name, most especially refusing to name ourselves, a radical sense of letting ourselves alone, without even the most subtle, internal self-bullying or coercion. It is the intimate experience in sitting alone by a fire, in silence and in reverie, with both a simplification and a growing clairvoyance of what is just beginning to be made known. A Winter of Listening.*

The Faces at Braga

In monastery darkness
by the light of one flashlight,
the old shrine room waits in silence.

While above the door
we see the terrible figure,
fierce eyes demanding, 'Will you step through?'

And the old monk leads us,
bent back nudging blackness,
prayer beads in the hand that beckons.

We light the butter lamps
and bow, eyes blinking in the
pungent smoke, look up without a word,

see faces in meditation,
a hundred faces carved above,
eye lines wrinkled in the hand-held light.

Such love in solid wood! Taken from the hillsides
and carved in silence, they have
the vibrant stillness of those who made them.

Engulfed by the past
they have been neglected, but through
smoke and darkness they are like the flowers

we have seen growing
through the dust of eroded slopes,
their slowly opening faces turned toward the mountain.

Carved in devotion, their eyes
have softened through age and their mouths
curve through delight of the carver's hand.

If only our own faces
would allow the invisible carver's hand
to bring the deep grain of love to the surface.

If only we knew
as the carver knew, how the flaws
in the wood led his searching chisel to the very core,

we would smile too
and not need faces immobilized
by fear and the weight of things undone.

When we fight with our failings, we ignore
the entrance to the shrine itself and wrestle
with the guardian, fierce figure on the side of good.

And as we fight
our eyes are hooded with grief
and our mouths are dry with pain.

If only we could give ourselves
to the blows of the carver's hands,
the lines in our faces would be the trace lines of rivers

feeding the sea
where voices meet, praising the features
of the mountain and the cloud and the sky.

Our faces would fall away
until we, growing younger toward death
every day, would gather all our flaws in celebration

to merge with them perfectly,
impossibly, wedded to our essence,
full of silence from the carver's hands.

THE FACES AT BRAGA *Placed firmly in my memory, a recollected collective experience of entering a then-remote monastery high in the Himalayas...In the darkness of the vestibule, waiting for one of our number to find the one flashlight we knew we had somewhere between us, I bumped into the carved temple guardian, or Vajrapani, with the same shock we might have bumping into a live person in the dark. The invitation in that encounter was to a robust living vulnerability, a willingness to embrace all difficulties and personal flaws as did the astonishingly carved, compassionate faces we found inside. Looking up at the carved figures, arrayed above us in the candlelight, I felt a revelatory wave of shock and a seeming recognition pass through us all. 'The Faces at Braga' was written to uncover the essence of that experience.*

The Sea in You

When I wake under the moon, I do not know
who I have become unless I move closer to you,
obeying the give and take of the earth as it breathes
the slender length of your body, so that in breathing
with the tide that breathes in you, and moving
with you as you come and go, and following you,
half in light and half in dark, I feel the first firm edge
of my floating palm touch and then trace the pale
light of your shoulder, to the faint moonlit shadow
of your smooth cheek, and drawing my finger through
the pearl water of your skin, I sense the breath
on your lips touch and then warm, the finest, furthest,
most unknown edge of my sense of self,
so that I come to you under the moon as if I had
swum under the deepest arch of the ocean,
to find you living where no one could possibly live,
and to feel you breathing where no one could possibly
breathe, and I touch your skin as I would
touch a pale whispering spirit of the tides, that my arms
try to hold with the wrong kind of strength and my
lips try to speak with the wrong kind of love and I follow
you through the ocean night listening for your breath
in my helpless calling to love you as I should, and I lie
next to you in my sleep as I would next to the sea,
overwhelmed by the rest that arrives in me and by
the weight that is taken from me and what, by morning,
is left on the shore of my waking joy.

Love in the Night

Sometimes when you lie close to me,
your body is so still in my arms
I find myself half in love with your
barely breathing form and half in love
with the unspeaking silent source
from which you come. I find myself
touching your lips with mine
to feel their warmth and bowing my head
to hear your breath, and stilling myself
to listen far inside you for the gentle rise
and fall of the tide that tells me
you are still free to come and go in life,
so that I take your hand in mine to sense
your pulse and touch your hair
and stroke your cheek and move my lips
to yours to feel the warmth emerging
from your inward self and to
see we are still here and still pledged
to breathe this world together.

All night like this I find myself asleep
and awake, turned toward the moon
and then turned toward you, your warmth
inviting me to bring you close
and leave you alone, all night I find myself
unable to choose between the love
I feel for you through closeness
and the grief of having to let you go
through distance, so that it seems
I can only breathe fully in the dark

by taking you in and giving you away
in your quiet rhythm of appearance
and disappearance, letting you return
in your breathing and not breathing,
or your half-sighed phrases spoken
to the dark, whispered from the dream
in which you live, so that I lie
between sleeping and waking,
seeing you are here and dreaming you are gone,
wanting to hold you and wanting to let you go,

living far inside you as you breathe close to me,
and living far beyond you, as I wait through
the hours of the night for you to wake
and find me again, the light in your eyes
half-dreaming on the pillow
looking back at me, and seeing me at last,

not knowing how far I have travelled,
through what distance I have come to find you,
where I have been, or what I have seen,
how far or how near; not knowing how
I have gained and lost you a hundred times
between darkness and dawn.

LOVE IN THE NIGHT *Falling in love is experienced physically like a real 'falling', the disorienting sense of ground giving way toward the mysterious tidal embrace of the other, or more disturbingly, falling toward a part of our self we had never quite understood, toward a form of happiness we often feel we do not deserve, and to a depth we did not feel we could venture to breathe in, 'as if swimming under the deepest arch of the ocean.' There is also a strange, tidal coming and going of edges and boundaries, influenced by everything it seems but our own will.*

In love we subvert the everyday structures of the life we had built so carefully and raze them to foundations on which a new, shared life can be built again. Unrequited love has its own form of fearful falling, but falling into a full felt and reciprocated love we face the most difficult, most revealing and most beautiful questions of all: are we large enough and generous enough and present enough; are we deserving enough, and ready enough to hold the joy, the future grief, and the overwhelming sense of privileged blessing that lies in that embrace?

To Break a Promise

Make a place of prayer, no fuss now,
just lean into the white brilliance
and say what you needed to say
all along, nothing too much, words
as simple and as yours and as heard
as the bird song above your head
or the river running gently beside you.

Let your words join one to another
the way stone nestles on stone,
the way water just leaves
and goes to the sea,
the way your promise
breathes and belongs
with every other promise
the world has ever made.

Now, let them go on,
leave your words
to carry their own life
without you, let the promise
go with the river.

Stand up now. Have faith. Walk away.

TO BREAK A PROMISE *Everywhere in our religious and artistic traditions, we are told how to make and hold to promises, and yet there is almost nothing in our literature to help us in the necessary art of breaking outworn, misguided, or out-of-season bonds that are now obscuring the underlying vow that led us to the commitment in the first place. Breaking promises is something most human beings have to do often, in order to remain true to the deeper underlying current of their lives and, just as often, the lives of those to whom they made the promise: but it is not something we often do well. This poem was written for a letting go that happened in the right kind of way, walking away from a promise that was no longer a promise for the future but an imprisoning bond to an abstract past.*

This poem could also live under the alternative title of 'To Make a Promise', a radical human act that calls for the same kind of leaning into the interior 'white brilliance' of truth as any promise we may have made. In the making of a necessary promise or in the necessary breaking of a promise, when we do find the core living words that speak for where we need to go or how we need to be, the words themselves have their own power, their own sweet way to take us on; and a need to be left alone to have their own life as a promise themselves, as an invitational mystery, an emblem of our courage, something thereafter to be lived up to and into.

Faith

I want to write about faith,
    about the way the moon rises
        over cold snow, night after night,

faithful even as it fades from fullness,
    slowly becoming that last curving and impossible
        sliver of light before the final darkness.

But I have no faith myself
    I refuse it even the smallest entry.

Let this then, my small poem,
    like a new moon, slender and barely open,
        be the first prayer that opens me to faith.

FAITH *'Faith' was written in a wondering moment, at the very beginning of my risking myself as 'a poet' in the world, in the daylight basement room of a friend's house; a wonder focused on the many disappearances which seemed to accompany my having stepped out along the uncharted vocational path as a full-time poet, whatever that mysterious term might mean. It was a way of reminding myself of the necessity for the 'radical simplifications' that only from the outside look like bravery. Most importantly, of the necessity for a friendship with the unknown that lay before me, held mythologically in both the interior darkness of our bodies and the body of the night sky by the way the moon first fades and then disappears completely for three days and nights of every month of every year of every life on this planet.*

The Well of Grief

Those who will not slip beneath
   the still surface on the well of grief,

turning down through its black water,
   to the place we cannot breathe,

will never know the source from which we drink,
   the secret water cold and clear,

nor find in the darkness glimmering,
   the small round coins,
      thrown by those who wished for something else.

THE WELL OF GRIEF *As a very serious young poet with a destination in mind, I decided to write a long and in-depth narrative poem on grief. There was an immediate physical sense of dropping down, dropping down through the body, dropping down through the gravitational pull of each line on the page, as if leaning down ever further to drink from a deeper source. Within six lines I caught a glimmer on the bottom of that well and despite my first attempts to ignore it, and to get back to my long epic, I knew the poem was over.*

All round the world, in all cultures we throw coins into wells to make a wish – this was the first time that I understood so physically that the wish is defensive and propitious. The essence of the wish is that we will be absolved from having to descend into the source ourselves. The coins take all kinds of forms, some of us have thrown marriages, friendships, hopes and dreams and, most of all, our necessary and robust vulnerabilities down there in the hope that the greater and more golden the sacrifice, the more it will absolve us from having to go down to that source – and a true physical and foundational understanding of the grief we carry with us. The Well of Grief.

Mameen

Be infinitesimal under that sky, a creature
even the sailing hawk misses, a wraith
among the rocks where the mist parts slowly.

Recall the way mere mortals are overwhelmed
by circumstance, how great reputations
dissolve with infirmity and how you,
in particular, stand a hairsbreadth from losing
everyone you hold dear.

Then, look back down the path to the north,
the way you came, as if seeing
your entire past and then south
over the hazy blue coast as if present
to a broad future.

Recall the way you are all possibilities
you can see and how you live best
as an appreciator of horizons
whether you reach them or not.

Admit, that once you have got up
from your chair and opened the door,
once you have walked out into the clear air
toward that edge and taken the path up high
beyond the ordinary, you have become

the privileged and the pilgrim,
the one who will tell the story
and the one, coming back
from the mountain
who helped to make it.

MAMEEN *In 'Deepest Connemara' in Ireland the veil seems*
very thin between this world and the next, between those
still living and those who have gone before us. The ancient
conversation between the mountains and the sea and the passing
sky magnifies one of the most extraordinary capabilities of
human beings: to hold many contexts and many conversations
and even many lives, lived and unlived together in one central
imagination. This poem is dedicated to John O'Donohue, who
first took me up to Mameen, as one who would introduce one
very good friend to another very good friend. John was one
who held enormous, wide-ranging, multi-layered contexts and
who still lives on as a companion to my imagination and my
everyday speech as much as he did when he could cast a shadow
and talk and walk and dream with me along the endless ridge
lines and shorelines between mountain and sea.

What to Remember when Waking

In that first
hardly noticed
moment
in which you wake,
coming back
to this life
from the other
more secret,
moveable
and frighteningly
honest
world
where everything
began,
there is a small
opening
into the day
that closes
the moment
you begin
your plans.

What you can plan
is too small
for you to live.

What you can live
wholeheartedly
will make plans

enough for the vitality
hidden in your sleep.

To become human
is to become visible
while carrying
what is hidden
as a gift to others.

To remember
the other world
in this world
is to live in your
true inheritance.

You are not
a troubled guest
on this earth,
you are not
an accident
amidst other accidents,
you were invited
from another and greater
night than the one
from which
you have just emerged.

Now, looking through
the slanting light
of the morning window
toward the mountain presence
of everything that can be,
what urgency
calls you
to your one love?

What shape
waits in the seed of you
to grow and spread
its branches
against a future sky?

Is it waiting
in the fertile sea?
In the trees
beyond the house?
In the life
you can imagine
for yourself?

In the open
and lovely
white page
on the waiting desk?

WHAT TO REMEMBER WHEN WAKING *looks at the crucial moment of re-entry into the physical world that astonishingly each of us experiences every morning of our waking. There is a whole cargo of revelation flowing out of that radically re-imagined state we call sleep, ready to inform the newly woken on even the most average workaday morning. Deep sleep is not only a revitalization of the body but a revolution of our sense of self and our understanding of the particular decisive threshold on which we now stand. Waking up into even the most ordinary day is a discipline, a test of our ability to hold the interior world, where we have just been re-imagined and revolutionized, with the moving, tidal, seasonal, not to be controlled, physical world we are just about to enter. What to Remember when Waking.*

Coleman's Bed

Make a nesting now, a place to which
the birds can come, think of Kevin's
prayerful palm holding the blackbird's egg
and be the one, looking out from this place
who warms interior forms into light.
Feel the way the cliff at your back
gives shelter to your outward view
and then bring in from those horizons
all discordant elements that seek a home.

Be taught now, among the trees and rocks,
how the discarded is woven into shelter,
learn the way things hidden and unspoken
slowly proclaim their voice in the world.
Find that far inward symmetry
to all outward appearances, apprentice
yourself to yourself, begin to welcome back
all you sent away, be a new annunciation,
make yourself a door through which
to be hospitable, even to the stranger in you.

See with every turning day,
how each season wants to make a child
of you again, wants you to become
a seeker after rainfall and birdsong,
watch now, how it weathers you to a testing
in the tried and true, tells you
with each falling leaf, to leave and slip away,
even from that branch that held you,

to go when you need to, to be courageous,
to be like that last word you'd want to say
before you leave the world.

Above all, be alone with it all,
a hiving off, a corner of silence
amidst the noise, refuse to talk,
even to yourself, and stay in this place
until the current of the story
is strong enough to float you out.

Ghost then, to where others
in this place have come before,
under the hazel, by the ruined chapel,
below the cave where Coleman slept,
become the source that makes
the river flow, and then the sea
beyond. Live in this place
as you were meant to, and then,
surprised by your abilities,
become the ancestor of it all,
the quiet, robust and blessed Saint
that your future happiness
will always remember.

COLEMAN'S BED *I was thirteen consecutive years visiting Saint Coleman's retreat in the Burren mountains of North Clare before I felt able to write this piece for this very, very invitational place: a cave and a ruined chapel nestled above the hazel wood, beside a fresh spring and sheltered by a limestone cliff. Coleman was a powerful agent of political and societal change, who helped not only to transform Irish society but post-Roman Europe, sending monks out from the Irish Church to form islands of cultural, contemplative and agricultural sanity into the most remote parts of a violent and beleaguered continent. The place and the life remembered are exemplary. This poem is written to represent the series of ever deeper questions that the place makes to each pilgrim visitor and looks at the way we settle best into a place in the same way we settle into our own bodies, as a series of invitations. The rested journey into the breath and the body we inhabit is the same pilgrimage we make into the outer landscape and body of the world. There is always an unspoken question behind every pilgrimage, an unspoken question I found answered in the lovely and surprising revelation that came to me at the end of the poem.*

The Seven Streams

Come down drenched, at the end of May,
with the cold rain so far into your bones
that nothing will warm you except your
own walking, and let the sun come out
at day's end near Slievenaglusha
with the rainbows doubling over Mulloch Mor
and see your clothes steaming in the bright air.

Be a provenance of something gathered,
a summation of previous intuitions,
let your vulnerabilities walking
on the cracked sliding limestone
be this time, not a weakness, but a faculty
for understanding what's about to happen.

Stand above the Seven Streams
letting the deep-down current surface
around you, then branch and branch
as they do, back into the mountain
and as if you were able for that flow,
say the few necessary words
and walk on, broader and cleansed
for having imagined.

THE SEVEN STREAMS   *The Seven Streams are a geo-*
graphical and mythological anomaly in a remote part of the
Burren mountains of North Clare; an ancient, difficult to find,
place of sanctity and healing. The water is pure, as is the air.
Cupping our hands to drink, we feel a far inward symmetry to all
this outer, thirst-quenching clarity emanating from the limestone
rock. The water appears from beneath a limestone escarpment,
creates a clear, wide pool, then meanders through a short, shallow
valley before disappearing, like our own lives, to appear again,
seemingly defying the laws of physics by reappearing as seven
separate flows beneath the cliff below. It is always a place that
points to what is essential, what must be uncovered, and what
must be let rest, to go its own way. The Seven Streams.

The House of Belonging

I awoke
this morning
in the gold light
turning this way
and that

thinking for
a moment
it was one
day
like any other.

But
the veil had gone
from my
darkened heart
and
I thought

it must have been the quiet
candlelight
that filled my room,

it must have been
the first
easy rhythm
with which I breathed
myself to sleep,

it must have been
the prayer I said
speaking to the otherness
of the night.

And
I thought
this is the good day
you could
meet your love,

this is the grey day
someone close
to you could die.

This is the day
you realize
how easily the thread
is broken
between this world
and the next

and I found myself
sitting up
in the quiet pathway
of light,

the tawny
close-grained cedar
burning round

me like fire
and all the angels
of this housely
heaven ascending
through the first
roof of light
the sun had made.

This is the bright home
in which I live,
this is where
I ask
my friends
to come,
this is where I want
to love all the things
it has taken me so long
to learn to love.

This is the temple
of my adult aloneness
and I belong
to that aloneness
as I belong to my life.

There is no house
like the house of belonging.

THE HOUSE OF BELONGING *One of the interesting dynamics of coming to ground, of suddenly having a sense of a real home and foundation again, is that it actually restores our relationship with the far, beckoning horizon of our life and gives us a proper sense of the future. This piece was begun to mark one of those powerful threshold experiences over which we seem to have no powers of personal manipulation. 'The House of Belonging' was written after waking up into a strong, almost tidal sense of new arrival in my life, a literal morning waking in a very old house that was very new to me, the weather of difficulty and heartache under which I had journeyed to get there swept away in the morning light, and the sudden realization that I was in a new place and in a new conversation with the future.*

The Opening of Eyes

That day I saw beneath dark clouds
the passing light over the water
and I heard the voice of the world speak out,
I knew then, as I had before
life is no passing memory of what has been
nor the remaining pages in a great book
waiting to be read.

It is the opening of eyes long closed.
It is the vision of far off things
seen for the silence they hold.
It is the heart after years
of secret conversing
speaking out loud in the clear air.

It is Moses in the desert
fallen to his knees before the lit bush.
It is the man throwing away his shoes
as if to enter heaven
and finding himself astonished,
opened at last,
fallen in love with solid ground.

THE OPENING OF EYES *Caught by a ray of light, something dramatically outlined in the outer world can find an equivalent deep-down symmetry inside us, as we look on, illuminating an as yet un-encountered part of ourselves, just beginning to make itself known, bringing inner and outer horizons together in one moment. This is the experience I had years ago, living in the mountains of Snowdonia, when I climbed the ridge behind my caravan to solve a difficult outer dilemma and reaching the top, looked over the sea toward Ireland. 'The Opening of Eyes', looks at the way that at any crucial moment in our life, there is never a choice between left or right, this way or that, it is always about taking a way forward that holds the two creatively together. In the midst of this understanding, the poem captures my new and flooding sense of something just about to be understood.*

Second Sight

Sometimes, you need the ocean light,
and colours you've never seen before
painted through an evening sky.

Sometimes you need your God
to be a simple invitation,
not a telling word of wisdom.

Sometimes you need only the first shyness
that comes from being shown things
far beyond your understanding,

so that you can fly and become free
by being still and by being still here.

And then there are times you need to be
brought to ground by touch
and touch alone.

To know those arms around you
and to make your home in the world
just by being wanted.

To see those eyes looking back at you,
as eyes should see you at last,

seeing you, as you always wanted to be seen,
seeing you, as you yourself
had always wanted to see the world.

SECOND SIGHT *The sense of the loved one seeing themselves through the intensity with which you are seeing them – and the reciprocation of that seeing – is the essence of the mutual, loving gaze. It is not confined to the merely human. Looking intensely at a landscape or the ocean, the give and take of the shoreline where the two meet, we fall in love, and perhaps equally, even find ourselves with a sense of being loved by the tidal essence of the world that we inhabit.*

The Truelove

There is a faith in loving fiercely
the one who is rightfully yours,
especially if you have
waited years and especially
if part of you never believed
you could deserve this
loved and beckoning hand
held out to you this way.

I am thinking of faith now
and the testaments of loneliness
and what we feel we are
worthy of in this world.

Years ago, in the Hebrides
I remember an old man
who walked every morning
on the grey stones
to the shore of the baying seals,

who would press his hat
to his chest in the blustering
salt wind and say his prayer
to the turbulent Jesus
hidden in the water,

and I think of the story
of the storm and everyone
waking and seeing
the distant

yet familiar figure
far across the water
calling to them,

and how we are all
preparing for that
abrupt waking,
and that calling,
and that moment
we have to say yes,
except it will
not come so grandly,
so Biblically,
but more subtly
and intimately in the face
of the one you know
you have to love,

so that when we finally
step out of the boat
toward them, we find
everything holds us
and everything confirms
our courage, and if you wanted
to drown you could,
but you don't
because finally
after all the struggle
and all the years,
you don't want to any more,

you've simply had enough
of drowning
and you want to live and you
want to love and you will
walk across any territory
and any darkness,
however fluid and however
dangerous, to take the
one hand you know
belongs in yours.

THE TRUELOVE *The beautiful surprise of arrival, having found the way opening before you into an overwhelming but marvelous invitation: across water, across new country, through another person's eyes, seeing and being seen inside and outside. A surface that before seemed hardly able to bear our weight, now a foundation.*

This poem has been recited now at hundreds of weddings around the world, most particularly for those for whom being visible in relationship, and most especially in marriage, was a courageous act in itself. It is more than a solace to the poet writing in a quiet, hermetic privacy, to have a few words become so beautifully and publicly communal.

Santiago

The road seen, then not seen, the hillside hiding
then revealing the way you should take, the road
dropping away from you as if leaving you to walk
on thin air, then catching you, holding you up,
when you thought you would fall, and the way
forward always in the end the way that you followed,
the way that carried you into your future, that brought
you to this place, no matter that it sometimes took
your promise from you, no matter that it had to break
your heart along the way: the sense of having walked
from far inside yourself out into the revelation,
to have risked yourself for something that seemed
to stand both inside you and far beyond you,
that called you back in the end to the only road
you could follow, walking as you did, in your rags
of love and speaking in the voice that by night
became a prayer for safe arrival, so that one day
you realized that what you wanted had already
happened, and long ago and in the dwelling place
in which you had lived in before you began,
and that every step along the way, you had carried
the heart and the mind and the promise
that first set you off and then drew you on
and that, you were more marvelous in your
simple wish to find a way than the gilded roofs
of any destination you could reach:
as if, all along, you had thought the end point
might be a city with golden domes, and cheering
crowds, and turning the corner at what you thought

was the end of the road, you found just a simple
reflection, and a clear revelation beneath the face
looking back and beneath it another invitation,
all in one glimpse: like a person or a place
you had sought forever, like a broad field of freedom
that beckoned you beyond; like another life,
and the road still stretching on.

SANTIAGO *'You were more marvelous in your simple wish to find a way': a line that might perhaps just encapsulate the ultimate form of faith: faith in the way we are made for the conversation; for the way we have taken, and that we look back upon, strangely only to see the path we took forward. The simple wish to find a way we can call our own through all the trials and tribulations and beautiful humiliations, and the radical act of daring to be happy along that way as we go.*

Finisterre

The road in the end taking the path the sun
had taken, into the western sea, and the moon
rising behind you, as you stood where ground
turned to ocean: no way to your future now
except the way your shadow could take, walking
before you across water, going where shadows go,
no way to make sense of a world that wouldn't
let you pass, except to call an end to the way
you had come, to take out each frayed letter
you had brought and light their illumined corners;
and to read them as they drifted on the late
western light: to empty your bags; to sort this
and to leave that; to promise what you needed to
promise all along, and to abandon the shoes
that brought you here right at the water's edge,
not because you had given up but because now
you would find a different way to tread,
and because, through it all, part of you would
still walk on, no matter how, over the waves.

FINISTERRE *My Irish niece (by ancient right of fosterage),*
Marlene McCormack, completed her studies in Irish drama
and set off into the world, not to teach drama, but to become
a dramatist herself, a vocational path for which one does not
receive much earthly corroboration in this life. Being good to
herself, she decided to begin this uncharted vocational path by
walking another parallel pilgrim path, the Camino de Santiago
de Compostela.

Driving in her company through a rainy night in Seattle
just after her completion of this 500-mile odyssey across
northern Spain, I asked her what the most powerful and
transformative moment had been on the entire trail. She replied
that it had been at the very end, after the city of Santiago,
reaching the wild edges of the Atlantic shore, at a place aptly
named Finisterre, The Ends of the Earth, and then she
described it in some detail. Fighting against the temptation to
pull over to the side of the road and start writing immediately, I
finished the poem at home at about two in the morning while
everyone was a-bed, including Marlene. I gave her the piece to
read at breakfast. Finisterre: The Ends of the Earth.

Everything is Waiting for You
(After Derek Mahon)

Your great mistake is to act the drama
as if you were alone. As if life
were a progressive and cunning crime
with no witness to the tiny hidden
transgressions. To feel abandoned is to deny
the intimacy of your surroundings. Surely,
even you, at times, have felt the grand array;
the swelling presence, and the chorus, crowding
out your solo voice. You must note
the way the soap dish enables you,
or the window latch grants you freedom.
Alertness is the hidden discipline of familiarity.
The stairs are your mentor of things
to come, the doors have always been there
to frighten you and invite you,
and the tiny speaker in the phone
is your dream-ladder to divinity.

Put down the weight of your aloneness and ease
into the conversation. The kettle is singing
even as it pours you a drink, the cooking pots
have left their arrogant aloofness and
seen the good in you at last. All the birds
and creatures of the world are unutterably
themselves. Everything is waiting for you.

EVERYTHING IS WAITING FOR YOU *The ancient intuition, corroborated only in our more profound states of attention and intentionality, of identity — not as a fixed or nameable commodity but more like a meeting, a call-and-answer song, a continual surprise. This surprising identity is one with equally surprising allies in the world, like the colour blue or a sudden doorway, or even a soap dish or a window latch — an identity that is enriched and deepened the more we pay attention to what is other than ourselves. Everything is Waiting for You.*

The Bell and the Blackbird

The sound
of a bell
still reverberating,

or a blackbird
calling
from a corner
of a field
asking you to wake
into this life
or inviting you
deeper,
into the one that waits.

Either way
takes courage,
either way wants you
to be nothing
but that self that
is no self at all,
wants you to walk
to the place
where you find
you already know
you'll have to give
every last thing
away.

The approach
that is also
the meeting
itself,
without any
meeting
at all.

That radiance
you have always
carried with you
as you walk
both alone
and completely
accompanied
in friendship
by every corner
of the world
crying
'Alleluia'.

Blessing for the Morning Light

The blessing of the morning light to you,
may it find you even in your invisible
appearances, may you be seen to have risen
from some other place you know and have known
in the darkness and that carries all you need.
May you see what is hidden in you as a place
of hospitality and shadowed shelter,
may what is hidden in you become your gift
to give, may you hold that shadow to the light
and the silence of that shelter to the word
of the light, may you join all of your previous
disappearances with this new appearance,
this new morning, this being seen again,
new and newly alive.

BLESSING FOR THE MORNING LIGHT *Perhaps there is nothing we take more for granted than the everyday light delineating our world and the faces of our loved ones, though sometimes we are tempted to appreciate only its ability to outline all our grounds for complaint. A reminder and a blessing, therefore, for those most basic ways; and at the same time those most astounding physical and beyond-physical ways that light forms our self-understandings and our perceptions of this world. Blessing for the Morning Light.*

A Seeming Stillness

We love the movement in a seeming stillness,
the breath in the body of the loved one sleeping,
the highest leaves in the silent wood,
a great migration in the sky above:
the waters of the earth, the blood in the body,
the first, soft, stir in the silence beneath a strident
voice, the internal hands of our mind,
always searching for touch, thoughts seeking other
thoughts, seeking other minds, the great arrival
of form through all our hidden themes.

And this breath, in this body, able,
just for a moment to give and to take,
to ask and be told, to find and be found,
to bless and be blessed, to hold and be held.

We are all a sun–lit moment come from
a long darkness, what moves us always
comes from what is hidden, what seems
to be said so suddenly has lived
in the body for a long, long time.

Our life like a breath, then, a give
and a take, a bridge, a central movement,
between singing a separate self
and learning to be selfless.

Breathe then, as if breathing for the first time,
as if remembering with what difficulty
you came into the world, what strength it took
to make that first impossible in-breath,
into a cry to be heard by the world.

Your essence has always been that first vulnerability
of being found, of being heard and of being seen,
and from the very beginning
the one who has always needed,
and been given, so much invisible help.

This is how you were when you first came
into the world, this is how you were
when you took your first breath in that world,
this is how you are now,
all unawares, in your new body and your new life,
this is the raw vulnerability of your every day,
and this is how you will want to be,
and be remembered, when you leave the world.

A SEEMING STILLNESS *One very still summer morning in Granada, Spain, waiting outside the coffee shop, Barista Durán – a place that may serve not only the very best coffee in Spain but also acts as my temporary morning writing studio – I found myself looking over the balustrade of the river Darro at a spreading tree whose highest leaves were being imperceptibly disturbed by the gentle breeze descending from the Sierra Nevada, like a river itself from mountains, and asking myself why, as human beings, we always find movement out of a seeming stillness so beautiful. Sitting to write inside the café, the image of a breathing loved one amidst the seeming stillness of sleep arrived first and the poem went on from there. A very memorable morning that concluded almost a year later in the same coffee shop, with lines entering a territory of sheer, raw, physical undoing, that surprised me, belying the poem's subtle beginnings.*

Fintan

The pool near Slane, where hazel brushes the gleam
of water and the just ripe nut touches and un-touches
the still cold darkness of a shaded stream, the wet
encircled shell a meniscus of light for the rising mouth
of a silvered salmon, scale and sleek. The moon,
the wait, the strike, the plash of dawn-lit water,
whoever ate this fish that fed on the tree of life,
whoever caught and cooked and then consumed
the flesh of the messenger-god, would make no king,
would uncover no gold to hoard against the coming
awe, would become mortal-wise through words
enfleshed with the nut of truth, would become equal
to the task of living and dying, a man acknowledged,
as one who *could* now speak for others, who *would* now
speak for others, greatest of poets in a land of poets.

is what we almost always are: close to happiness, close to one another, close to leaving, close to tears, close to God, close to losing faith, close to being done, close to saying something, or sometimes tantalizingly close to success, and even, with the greatest sense of satisfaction, close to giving the whole thing up.

Our human essence lies not in arrival, but in being almost there: we are creatures who are on our way, our journey a series of impending anticipated arrivals. We live by unconsciously measuring the inverse distances of our proximity: an intimacy calibrated by the vulnerability we feel in giving up our sense of separation.

To go beyond our normal identities and become closer than close is to lose our sense of self in temporary joy: a form of arrival that only opens us to deeper forms of intimacy that blur our fixed, controlling, surface identity.

To consciously become close is a courageous form of unilateral disarmament, a chancing of our arm and our love, a willingness to hazard our affections and an unconscious declaration that we might be equal to the inevitable loss that the vulnerability of being close will bring.

Human beings do not find their essence through fulfillment or eventual arrival but by staying close to the way they like to travel, to the way they hold the conversation between the ground on which they stand and the horizon to which they go. We are in effect, always close; always close to the ultimate secret: that we are more real in our simple wish to find a way than any destination we could reach: the step between not understanding that and understanding that, is as close as we get to happiness.

Hiding

is a way of staying alive. Hiding is a way of holding
ourselves until we are ready to come into the light.
Hiding is one of the brilliant and virtuoso practices of
almost every part of the natural world: the protective
quiet of an icy northern landscape, the held bud of a
future summer rose, the snow-bound internal pulse of
the hibernating bear. Hiding is underestimated. We
are hidden by life in our mother's womb until we grow
and ready ourselves for our first appearance in the
lighted world; to appear too early in that world is to
find ourselves with the immediate necessity for outside
intensive care.

Hiding done properly is the internal faithful
promise for a proper future emergence, as embryos, as
children or even as emerging adults in retreat from the
names that have caught us and imprisoned us, often in
ways where we have been too easily seen and too easily
named. We live in a time of the dissected soul, the
immediate disclosure; our thoughts, imaginings and
longings exposed to the light too much, too early and
too often, our best qualities squeezed too soon into a
world already awash with ideas that oppress our sense
of self and our sense of others. What is real is almost
always, to begin with, hidden and does not want to be
understood by the part of our mind that mistakenly
thinks it knows what is happening. What is precious
inside us does not care to be known by the mind in ways
that diminish its presence.

Hiding is an act of freedom from the misunder-
standing of others, especially in the enclosing world

of oppressive secret government and private entities, attempting to name us, to anticipate us, to leave us with no place to hide and grow in ways unmanaged by a creeping necessity for absolute naming, absolute tracking and absolute control. Hiding is a bid for independence, from others, from mistaken ideas we have about ourselves, from an oppressive and mistaken wish to keep us completely safe, completely ministered to, and therefore completely managed. Hiding is creative, necessary and beautifully subversive of outside interference and control. Hiding leaves life to itself, to become more of itself. Hiding is the radical independence necessary for our emergence into the light of a proper human future.

HIDING *I once found a fugitive little row boat hiding under branches, as if waiting for me to leap in and row it away, on the River Cong in County Mayo by the ruins of the old monastery that clings to its banks. It seemed to me to represent that deeply felt human need to creatively and subversively disappear; to turn away from the over-lighted human world and not be found so that we can actually catch up with ourselves and reappear in the world again more as we intuit we can be, possibly re-imagined, reinvigorated, regrown and rested; un-confined by the names we have accrued in the overly managed, human social worlds we are often forced to inhabit.*

To my mind, one of the great necessary inner disciplines is the ability to stay close to what is still hidden and unannounced in us, the interior 'deep but dazzling darkness' out of which any new and worthwhile future will be announced.

Despair

takes us in when we have nowhere else to go; when we feel the heart cannot break anymore, when our world or our loved ones disappear, when we feel we cannot be loved or do not deserve to be loved, when our God disappoints, or when our body is carrying profound pain in a way that does not seem to go away.

Despair is a haven with its own temporary form of beauty and of self-compassion, it is the invitation we accept when we want to remove ourselves from hurt.

Despair is a last protection. To disappear through despair, is to seek a temporary but necessary illusion, a place where we hope nothing can ever find us in the same way again.

Despair is a necessary and seasonal state of repair, a temporary healing absence, an internal physiological and psychological winter when our previous forms of participation in the world take a rest; it is a loss of horizon, it is the place we go to when we do not want to be found in the same way anymore. We give up hope when certain particular wishes are no longer able to come true and despair is the time in which we both endure and heal, even when we have not yet found the new form of hope.

Despair is strangely, the last bastion of hope; the wish being, that if we cannot be found in the old way, we cannot ever be touched or hurt in that way again. Despair is the sweet but illusory abstraction of leaving the body while still inhabiting it, so we can stop the body from feeling anymore. Despair is the place we go to when we no longer want to make a home in the world and where we feel, with a beautifully cruel form of satisfaction, that we may never have deserved that home in the first place. Despair, strangely, has its own sense of achievement, and despair, even more strangely, needs despair to keep it alive.

Despair turns to depression and abstraction when we try to make it stay beyond its appointed season and start to shape our identity around its frozen disappointments. But despair can only stay beyond its appointed time through the forced artificiality of created distance, by abstracting ourselves from bodily feeling, by trapping ourselves in the disappointed mind, by convincing ourselves that the seasons have stopped and can never turn again and, perhaps most simply and importantly, by refusing to let the body breathe by itself, fully and deeply. Despair is kept alive by freezing our sense of time and the rhythms of time; when we no longer feel imprisoned by time, and when the season is allowed to turn, despair cannot survive.

To keep despair alive, we have to abstract and immobilize our bodies, our faculties of hearing, touch and smell, and keep the surrounding springtime of the world at a distance. Despair needs a certain tending, a reinforcing, and isolation, but the body left to itself will breathe, the ears will hear the first birdsong of morning or catch the leaves being touched by the wind in the trees, and the wind will blow away even the grayest cloud; will move even the most immovable season; the heart will continue to beat and the world, we realize, will never stop or go away.

The antidote to despair is not to be found in the brave attempt to cheer ourselves up with happy abstracts, but in paying a profound and courageous attention to the body and the breath, independent of our imprisoning thoughts and stories – even, strangely, in paying attention to despair itself, and the way we hold it, and which we realize, was never ours to own and to hold in the first place. To see and experience despair fully in our body is to begin to see it as a necessary, seasonal visitation, and the first step in letting it have its own life, neither holding it nor moving it on before its time.

We take the first steps out of despair by taking on its full weight and coming fully to ground in our wish not to be here. We let our bodies and we let our world breathe again. In that place, strangely, despair cannot do anything but change into something else, into some other season, as it was meant to do, from the beginning. Despair is a difficult, beautiful necessity, a binding understanding between human beings caught in a fierce and difficult world where half of our experience is mediated by loss, but it is a season, a waveform passing through the body, not a prison surrounding us. A season left to itself will always move, however slowly, under its own patience, power and volition.

Refusing to despair about despair itself, we can let despair have its own natural life and take a first step onto the foundational ground of human compassion, the ability to see and understand and touch and even speak, the heartfelt grief of another.

DESPAIR *I am not a despairing person, and certainly, in the buoyancy of my present days I feel very, very far from that apparent state of giving in and giving up, but it was not too many years ago, telephone pressed against my ear, in the late night anonymity of a hotel room, hearing of the sudden loss of a close friend, that I felt the quiet hand of despair rest on my shoulder as she turned me resolutely to look her full in the face. In that giving over I felt for just a very few moments as if I had on my tongue, the unadulterated and unwanted pure malt taste of devastation and despair. It was a kind of fainting, and indeed I found myself a moment later, kneeling against the bed. I was astonished at the physical nature of the prostration, as if the body needed to give up holding its own weight, as if it simply couldn't hold its own weight anymore, as if it demanded to fall against something other than its own self; the way the forehead, that outer representation of the way we lead ourselves in thought, resting against the covers, simply did not want to be the one leading my thinking or knowing anymore.*

I was even more astonished to feel in that depth, how much of a different form of shelter and care waits for us beneath the outer forms of giving up, how that hand on the shoulder becomes a hand around the shoulder, and how a strange and marvelous mercy becomes available to us only in our sheer vulnerability, as if in stopping a certain way of holding the world I could allow myself to be held myself, in a different way. Despair, it seems, asks for its own difficult form of faith, extends its hand in a form of friendship we do not at first comprehend. It is as if as human beings, no matter its outward form, we find it impossible to live in the world without some sense of home; that even in despair we are able to find another beautiful form of shelter, a home at the core when all outer homes seem to have been stolen away.

Friendship

is a mirror to presence and a testament to forgiveness. Friendship not only helps us see ourselves through another's eyes, but can be sustained over the years only with someone who has repeatedly forgiven us for our trespasses as we must find it in ourselves to forgive them in turn. A friend knows our difficulties and shadows and remains in sight, a companion to our vulnerabilities more than our triumphs, when we are under the strange illusion we do not need them. An undercurrent of real friendship is a blessing exactly because its elemental form is rediscovered again and again through understanding and mercy. All friendships of any length are based on a continued, mutual forgiveness. Without tolerance and mercy all friendships die.

Friendship is the great hidden transmuter of all relationship: it can transform a troubled marriage, make honorable a professional rivalry, make sense of heartbreak and unrequited love and become the newly discovered ground for a mature parent–child relationship.

The dynamic of friendship is almost always underestimated as a constant force in human life: a diminishing circle of friends is the first terrible diagnostic of a life in deep trouble: of overwork, of too much emphasis on a professional identity, of forgetting who will be there when our armored personalities run into the inevitable natural disasters and vulnerabilities found in even the most average existence.

Through the eyes of a friend we especially learn to remain at least a little interesting to others. When we flatten our personalities and lose our curiosity in the life of the world or of another, friendship loses spirit and animation; boredom is the second great killer of friendship. Through the natural surprises of a relationship held through the passage of years we recognize the greater surprising circles of which we are a part and the faithfulness that sustains a wider sense of revelation, independent of human relationship: to learn to be friends with the earth and the sky, with the horizon and with the seasons, even with the disappearances of winter, and in that faithfulness take the difficult path of becoming a good friend to our own going.

Friendship transcends disappearance: an enduring friendship goes on after death, the exchange only transmuted by absence, the relationship advancing and maturing in a silent internal conversational way even after one half of the bond has passed on.

But no matter the medicinal virtues of being a true friend or sustaining a long close relationship with another, the ultimate touchstone of friendship is not improvement, neither of the self nor of the other; the ultimate touchstone is witness: the privilege of having been seen by someone and the equal privilege of being granted the sight of the essence of another, to have walked with them and to have believed in them, and sometimes just to have accompanied them for however brief a span, on a journey impossible to accomplish alone.

is unpreventable; the natural outcome of caring for people and things over which we have no control, of holding in our affections those who inevitably move beyond our line of sight. Even the longest, strongest marriage has had its heart broken many times just in the act of staying together.

Heartbreak begins the moment we are asked to let go but cannot: in other words, it colours and inhabits and magnifies each and every day; heartbreak is not a visitation, but a path that human beings follow through even the most average life. Heartbreak is an indication of our sincerity: in a love relationship, in a life's work, in trying to learn a musical instrument, in the attempt to shape a better more generous self. Heartbreak is the beautifully helpless side of love and affection and is just as much an essence and emblem of care as the spiritual athlete's quick but abstract ability to let go. Heartbreak has its own way of inhabiting time and its own beautiful and trying patience in coming and going.

Heartbreak is how we mature; yet we use the word heartbreak as if it only occurs when things have gone wrong: an unrequited love, a shattered dream, a child lost before their time. Heartbreak, we hope, is something we hope we can avoid; something to guard against, a chasm to be carefully looked for and then walked around; the hope is to find a way to place our feet where the elemental forces of life will keep us in the manner to which we want to be accustomed and which will keep us from the losses that all other human beings have experienced without exception since the beginning of conscious time. But heartbreak may be the very essence of being human, of being on the journey from here to there, and of coming to care deeply for what we find along the way.

If heartbreak is inevitable and inescapable, our only choice might be to look for it and make friends with it, to see it as our constant and instructive companion, and even perhaps, in the depth of its impact as well as in its hindsight, to see it as its own reward.

Heartbreak asks us not to look for an alternative path, because there is no alternative path. It is a deeper introduction to what we love and have loved, an inescapable and often beautiful question, something or someone who has been with us all along, asking us to be ready to let go of the way we are holding things and preparation perhaps, for the last letting go of all.

HEARTBREAK *We tend to think of 'enlightenment' as an abstract, as being a state above all suffering, but Buddha asked his followers in very intimate terms to follow heartbreak to its very end, to see it as part of any ultimate understanding, in effect to say the very last goodbye, to be completely present to 'everything ceasing', to everything we are constantly being asked to let go of, to the very origin of our pain, and thereby to let it flower into something else. My wife and I ran into this lovely family group for only a very brief train ride through the mountains of central Japan, but the chemistry and poignancy of the encounter and the tidal manner in which they suddenly had to leave, and the image they left in my camera, waving to us from an obscure country station platform, seemed to embody all the hellos and goodbyes I had ever made.*

is always surprisingly new to those actually growing older, the stranger in the mirror a mortal testament to the rigours of a journey that someone we seem to know has undergone, but somehow also a reflection that is never a true outer representation of the new, inner life just in the act of being born, far inside us. The fact that we are surprised by age might be the most surprising fact of all. Advancing age, whether we are thirty five or seventy five, is always extraordinarily and strangely fresh in its appearance – and age always does take us by surprise – both in the mild shock of seeing ourselves, as if for the first time, in the passing shop window but also in how others deign to treat us, addressing not our sense of true self but a self they have assigned to the outline we make, to certain behaviours, to certain misconceptions we are also troubled to think, we might be unconsciously reinforcing.

Age is an accusation in the court of mortality, and there is a solid, foundational part of us sure we have been unjustly and purposefully framed and are standing before both judge and jury perfectly innocent of the crime. We look into the mirror and do not see a proper representation of what we experience of our inner selves, we actually see someone who seems to have committed a felony on our behalf: we feel we are subject to guilt by association; we see the reflection of some untrustworthy individual on the outside that we have unconsciously aided and abetted, someone we may have accompanied from the inside out, but someone we know only at a strange distance: someone telling the world, who might have made the diffcult journey on the outside, buffeted by wind, weather and heartbreak; what they might have suffered through making it, what hurt them and what wore them down over the years, but nothing of the new complexion emerging from within, that we intuit, is our real self; a self that seems to carry only some kind of necessary innocence for the unknown journey waiting just beyond our present grasp.

Old is never us, and the intuition may be a true one. Even in the vulnerabilities that occur approaching death, the mind and body revisit and re-inhabit the younger body and the younger self we lived, shrugging off in that living memory, any disease or the layered years of burden. The essence of a human life might be just getting ready to be ready. Every new measure of our increasing age, whether eighteen or eighty, seems to demand a new inhabitation of youthfulness, independent of outer form: a sense of standing at a new threshold, without which our future life withers under trembling fears that tend to be dressed up as a wisely gathered cynicism.

Old is a necessary shedding, not only of the need to have a younger, outer athletic body, but the shedding of the way we have understood age itself. We may anticipate being 'Old' as denoting a closing down, but we may only be closing down because at the core we feel everything more keenly than we ever did in our younger, immature and immortal days. Age, eldership and an ever keener physical sense in our memory of successive heartbreaks, combined with the bodily understanding of our increasing vulnerability, can have us experiencing life like a heartbroken adolescent once again.

The only cure for personal heartbreak is a greater trans-personal context, and we might say, a greater sense of humour, and thus, the puzzling accusation of being old, asks us to learn to live again as a different kind of witness to the disappointment living in our reflected face, or in a daughter's face, or in the many faces of our society: we understand at a deeper level, the inevitable heartbreak of a loved one we are powerless to help, and that at times, we cannot even help ourselves, except through a deeper sense of witness, except through our companionship and compassion: made all the more powerful by refusing to give others, or ourselves, easy, gratuitous advice.

Ageing is our apprenticeship to both increasing presence and increasing disappearance, at one and the same time. Just as we could never fully understand in our twenties, who we would become in our fifties, we come to know, whether we are believer or unbeliever, that we will never understand fully who or what we will find on the other side of the veil. We give up on the purely visible in order to go on in a different more invisible way.

Age and maturity at their most admired, always

combine to create a fine sense of humour about who we are, who we were and what we actually contributed to others; a gathering sense that even with a massive reservoir of cash we may have built in our retirement accounts, the rest of creation might very well be relieved to see us go earlier rather than later in the universal program of events: to make way for something less guarded, less defended, less abstracted and a little more willing to be a miracle that risks itself amongst all the other miracles of life. It may be instructive to think that creation seems to have taken a magnificent risk with our first appearance on this earth and might be just that little bit disappointed, once we stop risking ourselves in a manner equally to be admired.

'Old' transforms, transmutes and transfigures desire. Eros and attraction do not fall away with age – desire stays alive – more intriguing for the quicksilver manner of its transformation: the axis of attraction only moves, from the outer complexion in its attempts to call in other bodies and other lives, to an inner axis of attraction, an inner complexion, calling not only for physical union but a meeting with a greater invisible body that we intuit has awaited us all along: that is, our inherited, birthright, physical and strangely non-physical sense of belonging to the ageless.

Those desires we often followed – growing into life – the car as a signal of our glamorous powers – the unused boat as something we can constantly mention –

the second home that keeps our holidays just as busy as our home life – are all suddenly seen to have been, not doorways to adventure, but shields against any true, inner discovery, and all, in the end, too narrow, too ungenerous, and even strangely absurd. We realise that many of the objects we thought of as the natural gifts of an earned maturity were simply new toys appropriate only to what we now understand as a second infancy.

Age without maturity is always the second helplessness of a childhood much worse than the first one. Age combined with maturity not only holds childhood's core understanding of play itself as being far more important than any particular toy, but most especially, age combined with an earned maturity combines youth's precious and visionary relationship with the future; most especially with a future it cannot as yet fully understand.

Youth has the burning need to travel from the here and now to the there and then, 'Old' has the possibility of understanding, that no matter where it finds itself in the world, 'here and now'; is the biggest, most challenging, and most interesting journey of all, demanding everything for a proper arrival.

No matter whether we are called 'Old' or not; no matter our chronological age; at thirty or even, in our not too distant future, at a hundred and thirty – in the midst of our life or at the shoreline of our death – at the very centre of all the edges and unattractive horizons that have us hesitating at the word 'Old' there can burn

the rose fire of an inner compass, hidden perhaps
for so long, but now despite every outer diffculty or
disappearance, able to blossom with new and strangely
youthful directions.

'Old' is not a state that replaces the word 'Young',
but a fierce and uncompromising invitation to an
earned experience of an ever youthful essence.

Your Prayer

only began
with words,

each one
you realize

just
a hand
on the door
to silence,

each one,
just you
leaning your
full weight
against everything
you felt
you could never
deserve,

even
in your
gathered
chanted strength

what you said
in the end
was only
a shoulder

against the grain
of wood

trying to keep
the entrance
open,

until that door
which
had been no door
at all
gave in

to necessary
grief,
which is really
only the full
understanding
of what
you were missing
all along,
which

is really
just that
vulnerability
you needed
to make
a proper
invitation,

which is really
just you
admitting
the full depth
of your love at last.

The heart-broken
heart
coming to
heartfelt rest

the opening
inside you
now filled to the
gleaming brim
and
casting
its generous beam,

the part of you
you thought
was foolish,
the wisest voice of all.

This poem marks an experience that in many ways initiated the whole cycle of experiences laid out so physically in this book: witnessing the death-bed monologue of a monk at Mount Saint Bernard Abbey, in the North of England, saying he had 'given up' praying years ago. The first thought, in witnessing his testimony, was that he had lost his faith — only to hear him then say that he had given up praying because his whole life had become a living breathing prayer, that he had lived and indeed breathed from the atmosphere of prayer for years, whether that atmosphere was given words or not.

The Edge You Carry With You

What is this
beguiling reluctance
to be happy?

This quickness
in turning away
the moment
you might
arrive?

The felt sense,
that a moment's
unguarded joy
might after all,
just kill you?

You know
so very well
the edge
of darkness
you have
always
carried with you.

You know
so very well,
your childhood legacy:
that particular,
inherited
sense of hurt,

given to you
so freely
by the world
you entered.

And you know
too well
by now
the body's
hesitation
at the invitation
to undo
everything
others seemed
to want to
make you learn.

But your edge
of darkness
has always
made
its own definition
secretly
as an edge
of understanding

and the door
you closed
might,
by its very nature,

be
one just waiting
to be leant against
and opened.

And happiness
might just
be a single step away,
on the other side
of that next
unhelpful
and undeserving
thought.

Your way home,
understood now,
not as an achievement,
but as a giving up,
a blessed undoing,
an arrival
in the body
and a full rest
in the give
and take
of the breath.

This living
breathing body
always waiting
to greet you

at the door,
always prepared
to give you
the rest you need,

always,
no matter
the long
years away,
still
wanting you,
to come home.

For the Road to Santiago

For the road to Santiago,
don't make new declarations
about what to bring
and what to leave behind.

Bring what you have.

You were always going
that way anyway,
you were always
going there all along.

Afterword

Long before I fell in love with the man, I fell in love
with the poet for the way his words create an opening
for all of us to find our own way into a sense of ground
and home in our bodies and experiences, while casting
a larger horizon to move into our future all at once.

As I was struggling up the Inca Trail in the mountains of Peru one birthday, many years ago, memorizing
'Everything is Waiting for You' (and cursing the many
stairs that were indeed my 'mentor of things to come'),
I carried a hastily scrawled, handwritten copy on a torn
notebook page. A book such as the one you are reading
would have fit perfectly in my pilgrim rucksack, a
companion to the journey in the way that one wants to
have a treasured friend and companion along the road.

I chose these poems because they have guided me
through many difficult years – some lines becoming
mantras for more boldly inhabiting a desired way
of being in the world, helping me as I read, 'let
your vulnerabilities walking on the cracked sliding
limestone be this time, not a weakness, but a faculty for
understanding what's about to happen'.

The poems and essays collectively ask us to live fully
into each epoch of our lives – into the daily shifts, the
ever-turning seasonalities, and the broader cycles of
gain and grief that are a part of our maturation, native
to every phase of life and every person.

The poems are both for the times of day when we
experience the world through its nuanced shadings and
transitions, and also for the seasons when the colorations

of the sky and earth turn more radically through darkness and light.

These poems are also offered within the context of an epoch when our human spirits and imaginations need all the support they can get. In this time of great light and great darkness, volatility and change, rapid technological, geopolitical, and economic shifts, as David Whyte says, 'Each of us will be asked to reach deeper, speak more bravely, live more from the fierce perspectives of the poetic imagination; to find the lines, in effect, already written inside us: poetry does not take surface political sides, it is always the conversation neither side is having, it is the breath in the voice about to discover itself only as it begins to speak, and it is that voice firmly anchored in a real and touchable body, standing on the ground of our real, inhabited world, speaking from a source that lives and thrives at that threshold between opposing sides we call a society'.[1]

GAYLE KAREN YOUNG WHYTE
Langley
August 2019

[1] From David's 'Letter from the House 2017', www.davidwhyte.com

Photo Credits